MILLENNIAl

Jack Randall Glad

Copyright © 2024 JACK GLAD

All Rights Reserved

Dedication

To my son,

I have watched you fade in—growing stronger, wiser, and more remarkable with each passing day. Someday, you will watch me fade out. But know that as life moves forward, my love for you will remain as steady as ever.

All I ask is that you chase your dreams fearlessly. Live boldly, love deeply, and never let go of the fire that drives you. I will always be with you, cheering you on and proud of the man you are becoming.

With love from the bottom of my heart,

Dad

About the Author

Jack Glad is the Weapons Flight Chief for the 122d Fighter Wing, Indiana Air National Guard, with over 17 years of dedicated service to his country. In his current role, Sergeant Glad is responsible for supervising and mentoring a team of Airmen, ensuring the meticulous maintenance and operational readiness of weapons systems on A-10C and F-16 aircraft. Known for his exceptional leadership and technical proficiency, Jack has played a key role in the mission success of the 122d Fighter Wing.

Jack enlisted in the Air National Guard in June 2007, motivated by a desire to serve his nation. He completed his technical training at Sheppard Air Force Base in Texas, where he honed his skills in aircraft maintenance and weapons systems. Following his training, he was assigned to the 122d Aircraft Maintenance Squadron, quickly rising through the ranks due to his commitment, skill, and dedication. His career has seen him deploy in support of Operations ENDURING FREEDOM and INHERENT RESOLVE, where he contributed to critical missions, demonstrating his steadfast commitment to national defense.

Beyond his military achievements, Jack's life took a transformative turn in 2016 when he became a father. This new chapter brought a profound sense of purpose and fulfillment, influencing both his personal and professional life. Jack's journey as a father has deepened his understanding of leadership, patience, and resilience—qualities he brings to his role in the Air National Guard.

Jack Glad's diverse background spans both military and civilian roles, reflecting a well-rounded individual with a strong work ethic, technical expertise, and an unwavering dedication to excellence. Whether leading a team of Airmen or balancing the demands of fatherhood, Jack embodies the core values of integrity, service, and excellence. His story is one of resilience, commitment, and a relentless drive to serve his country and family with honor.

Preface

Life has a way of testing us in ways we never see coming. As a family, we've faced our share of struggles—more than most might ever know. Yet, through every hardship, challenge, and moment of doubt, we've endured. This book is not just a reflection on those hard times but a testament to the love that has kept us going, even when things seemed impossible.

I know we haven't always had it easy. We've weathered storms that could have torn us apart, but here we are—still standing, still fighting, still together. In all those difficult moments, my love for you has never wavered. It's only grown stronger. Through every argument, every tear, every setback, I've seen the strength and resilience of our family. And no matter what we've gone through, I want you to know that I am proud of us, proud of you, and proud of the love that binds us. This book is my way of acknowledging the pain and challenges we've faced, but more importantly, it's a tribute to the love that has endured. We may not be perfect, but we are real, and I wouldn't trade our journey for anything. Family is about sticking together, no matter what—and that's exactly what we've done.

You'll be in my heart, Bad Boys for life, Jack and Bert show, Why Knot, and the Armor of God!

With all my heart,

Jack Glad

Contents

Dedication i

About the Author ii

Preface iv

Chapter 1: Mental Resilience 1

Chapter 2: Boy on the Curb 12

Chapter 3: Leaving on an Airplane 22

Chapter 4: The Battle of Custody 37

Chapter 5: Second Deployment 52

Chapter 6: The Puzzle Piece 64

Chapter 7: Life Goes On 77

Instead of the better world we envisioned, we all got slammed with debt, employment issues, and an unstable future. Very few of us managed to claw our way out of the void we were thrown into due to the world slowly approaching its demise. But what helped those few people to still hold on and not get swept away with the tides of distress?

It was mental resilience.

Mental resilience is to pull yourself back up after adversity and face the challenges life throws at you in the best possible way. It is a practice of regulating your thoughts and garnering your inner strength to help you overcome obstacles and emerge stronger than ever before.

For my generation, mental resilience is very important. It is a tool that became our salvation, an anchor that kept us rooted to sanity. Those who didn't use it suffered and couldn't pull themselves out of the claws of recession and other instabilities.

It is crucial even for today's world as so much is going on, and we have so many different opinions shoved in our faces. Having access to social media has made us insecure and forget about the true essence of life. We are always aware of everything and have access to so many people and profiles that we seem to chase an illusion.

An illusion of happiness, contention, a life that is picture perfect.

Inspired by these mirages, we often undermine our own achievements and feel insecure about the lives we lead. We chase after an ideal that is far from normal simply because it appears to be so through the curated and filtered screens of our phones. This relentless pursuit of illusionary perfection can leave us feeling inadequate and dissatisfied.

Reflecting on life twenty years before the advent of pervasive technology, we see a stark contrast. Our ancestors, as they worked diligently to build their futures, lived within a more contained and tangible social bubble. Their worlds were smaller, and their interactions were limited to those within their immediate reach—family, friends, and local community members. They seldom needed to venture beyond these familiar social circles to seek validation or connection. Their expectations were markedly different from ours today. Without the constant barrage of images and narratives showcasing others' seemingly perfect lives, their own lives were framed by the immediate realities they faced. This simplicity often translated into a form of contentment that is rare in today's hyper-connected world. Their lives, though they might seem mundane or even monotonous by our modern standards, were often filled with a sense of fulfillment and happiness. This was largely because they were not constantly comparing their lives to an endless stream of idealized representations but were instead rooted in the tangible, day-to-day experiences that made up their reality.

The absence of widespread technology meant that the pressures of keeping up with an ever-expanding array of social expectations were minimal. The joy of everyday accomplishments was not overshadowed by the unattainable standards set by a global digital audience. In this more insular world, people could find satisfaction in the simple things—gathering with loved ones, engaging in meaningful work, and participating in community life. Their aspirations were more grounded, their achievements more personal, and their sense of identity more securely tied to their immediate social environment.

Our modern lives are often dominated by a constant stream of digital content that can distort our perceptions of what is normal and desirable. This can lead to an endless cycle of striving for an ever-elusive ideal, leaving us feeling perpetually unfulfilled. By looking back at how our ancestors lived, we might find valuable lessons in finding contentment within the bounds of our own realities rather than in the unrealistic comparisons that technology often compels us to make.

Fast forward to the present, where our lives are surrounded by too many expectations, too little time, and the burden of making ends meet despite the heavy inflation. The Internet gave us access to every person's point of view, and the more people we interact with, the more we are influenced by their opinions and perceptions. Ever since the advent of social media, our values have changed as our lives are directed by what we see on our phones. We got swept up by the image of what a man, woman, or child should look or behave like. The way other people led their lives (or, in some cases, pretended to lead their lives) indirectly shaped us to be like them, too. It increased the pressure we were already experiencing, and the fear of missing out dug its claws deep inside our shaking hearts.

Furthermore, the economy started to go down. Jobs became stagnated, and managing finances became even tougher than earlier.

In such troubling times, we must focus on training ourselves to be mentally resilient.

Mental resilience is not necessarily a trait you are born with. It can be acquired through time, and you can train yourself to be resilient in the face of adversity. You can cope with the pain and trauma life has dealt you with over the years by strengthening your inner self and recognizing what your inner voice says to you. The concept of connecting with yourself and cultivating mental resilience inspired me to write this book.

I wish to spread the important message of embracing mental resilience as a key to achieving success. In a world filled with pessimistic news about looming catastrophes, the end of days, or the rapid passage of time, it's easy to feel overwhelmed and defeated. However, despite all the negativity that surrounds us, it is crucial to remember that it is never too late to make a positive change in yourself.

Mental resilience is the strength that allows us to navigate through life's challenges, bounce back from setbacks, and continue moving forward with hope and determination. It is about developing the capacity to withstand adversity, recover quickly from difficulties, and maintain a positive outlook even in the face of hardship. This resilience is not something we are born with; it is a skill that can be cultivated through practice, self-awareness, and a commitment to personal growth.

By focusing on building mental resilience, we empower ourselves to take control of our lives. We learn to manage stress more effectively, to adapt to changing circumstances, and to find solutions to problems that might otherwise seem insurmountable. This mindset not only enhances our ability to cope with immediate challenges but also prepares us for future obstacles, making us more robust and capable individuals. In addition to personal benefits, embracing mental resilience can also have a ripple effect on those around us. When we demonstrate resilience, we inspire others to do the same. Our strength and positivity can serve as a beacon of hope for friends, family, and colleagues who may be struggling with their own challenges. By fostering a culture of resilience, we contribute to the overall well-being of our communities and create an environment where positive change is possible for everyone.

Change is always possible. It is never too late to start working on yourself, develop mental resilience, and embrace a more positive and proactive approach to life. By doing so, you not only enhance your own quality of life but also contribute to a more resilient and hopeful world.

You must have heard the saying: "Pain is inevitable; suffering is optional."

Pain exists in different forms for all of us, but how we choose to deal with it defines us as resilient or doomed people. If we let suffering take hold, we doom ourselves to a point of no return—a dark and hopeless fate.

However, those who face these hardships head-on and turn their lives around through their inner strength emerge stronger than ever before, ultimately achieving their dreams. They become living testaments to the idea that the strongest swords are forged in the hottest fires. Pain and trauma become the forging fire of their lives, and they use the lessons learned from those trying times to craft a better, more resilient future.

In the midst of adversity, these individuals demonstrate an incredible capacity for growth and transformation. Instead of succumbing to despair or allowing setbacks to define them, they tap into their inner reserves of strength and determination. This process is not easy; it requires immense courage, perseverance, and a willingness to confront one's deepest fears and challenges. Yet, it is through this very struggle that they find the power to reinvent themselves and their circumstances. As they navigate through their trials, they develop invaluable skills and insights that serve them well in their journey. They learn to manage their emotions, stay focused on their goals despite distractions and obstacles, and adapt to changing situations with grace and ingenuity.

These experiences cultivate a deep sense of resilience and resourcefulness, enabling them to tackle future challenges with greater confidence and capability. The transformation that occurs through overcoming adversity often leads to a profound shift in perspective. These individuals gain a greater appreciation for the value of persistence and the importance of maintaining a positive outlook, even in the face of hardship. They come to understand that setbacks are not the end but rather opportunities for growth and self-improvement. This newfound perspective empowers them to pursue their dreams with renewed vigor and a deeper sense of purpose.

The journey of turning pain and trauma into a source of strength also fosters a sense of empathy and compassion. Having experienced profound difficulties themselves, they become more attuned to the struggles of others and more willing to offer support and encouragement. This creates a ripple effect, where their resilience and positive transformation inspire those around them to also strive for better and to believe in their own potential for change.

Ultimately, these individuals serve as powerful examples of the human spirit's capacity to overcome and thrive. They show us that it is possible to turn even the most challenging experiences into stepping stones toward a brighter future. By facing their hardships head-on and harnessing the lessons learned from their trials, they not only achieve their own dreams but also pave the way for others to follow in their footsteps. Their stories remind us that, no matter how difficult our circumstances may be, we have the power within us to forge a better future and emerge stronger, wiser, and more resilient than ever before.

You can do that, too, if you vow to be true to yourself and harness your inner strength. Consider each struggle in life as an objective to complete rather than a problem to run away from. The experience you gain as a result levels up your character and prepares you for future battles. Think of yourself as a warrior and your life as a battlefield. You will go through highs and lows and experience the worst points of your life, but what matters most is that you must pick yourself up like a true warrior who never gives up.

Through my personal experience, I wish to educate young readers and fellow millennials on how this mindset changed my life and made me better equipped to deal with everything I have gone through till now. I want to spread the word that you must love yourself and connect with your soul to be strong and resilient. The stronger connection you build with your inner self, the easier it becomes for you to overcome the challenges of your life.

The world we inherited was far from the utopia we envisioned. Instead, we have faced numerous challenges and adversities that our predecessors could hardly have imagined. Despite these obstacles, our generation defies the myths and stereotypes often associated with us. We have not only survived but thrived, even when many expected us to fail. We are survivors, warriors in our own right, demonstrating time and again our resilience and determination.

Through this book, I want us all to come together and support one another in our quest to become better versions of ourselves. This is not just about personal growth but about collective transformation. We have the power to change our circumstances and reshape the world into a place that reflects our highest ideals and aspirations.

By cultivating strength and mental resilience, we can equip ourselves to handle whatever life throws our way. These qualities are not just about enduring hardships; they are about thriving in the face of them. Mental resilience enables us to bounce back from setbacks, learn from our experiences, and continue moving forward with a sense of purpose and optimism. Imagine a generation united by a common goal of self-improvement and mutual support. Together, we can create a ripple effect of positive change, inspiring others to join us in our efforts. Our collective strength can drive the social, cultural, and technological advancements needed to build a better future. This is not just a dream; it is a possibility that we can realize through our combined efforts and shared vision.

We must also recognize that the change we seek starts within us. By focusing on our own development and well-being, we set the stage for broader societal transformation. When we become strong and mentally resilient, we become catalysts for change, capable of influencing and uplifting those around us. Our inner strength becomes a beacon of hope and inspiration, encouraging others to embark on their own journeys of growth and self-discovery.

By banding together and supporting one another, we can overcome the pessimism and doubt that often surrounds us. We can prove that our generation is not defined by the challenges we face but by how we respond to them. We have the capacity to create a legacy of resilience, innovation, and positive change that will benefit future generations.

So, let us embrace this journey with courage and determination. Let us commit to becoming the best versions of ourselves, not just for our own sake but for the sake of the world we wish to build. Together, as survivors and warriors, we can bring about the change that has always been expected from us. Our potential is limitless, and our future is in our hands.

So, let's join hands, embrace our challenges, and cultivate our inner strengths. Together, we can build the future we deserve.

Chapter 2: Boy on the Curb

"Childhood is a promise that is never kept."

—Ken Hill

Childhood is a time many of us recall with a blend of sweetness and sorrow. Every memory from those years carries a bittersweet tinge, evoking a sense of longing to return to a simpler, more innocent time. It was a period when the pressures of responsibility were nonexistent, and our imaginations thrived on the belief in fairies, magic, and endless possibilities.

The enchantment of those days, when life felt like an unending adventure, often leads us to yearn for a return to that innocence and wonder. This nostalgic longing, this desire to revisit the carefree moments of our youth, is a common sentiment shared by many. As we grow older, the reality of adulthood and its myriad responsibilities can sometimes make us wistfully reminisce about the magic and simplicity of our childhood.

However, childhood is a fractured collection of a few of the memories that I didn't trauma block. Isn't it strange that our brain takes hold of our memories and blocks them completely if we experience something traumatic or with a lasting impact?

I don't remember much of my childhood, but I would like to share a few memories that weren't wiped out. These memories make up the patchwork of my childhood. Like different pieces of cloth sewn together to form a brightly colored rug, my childhood was a collection of all these diverse experiences.

An early memory that I want to share is the first time I got dropped off to live with my Dad at his place. My parents divorced when I was three; since then, I lived with my Mom. I was six years old, and my mom's house was all I knew— all I could associate with the concept of being home. Since I grew up without seeing my mom and dad together, I felt it was normal for my parents to live separately. I never even asked my Mom the reason for their separation. Perhaps it didn't matter back then.

However, at the tender ag of six, when the first drop-off to my father's place occurred, I realized that my world had split in two and would be divided between my mother and father.

All I knew was that I was in the backseat of my mom's silver Thunderbird, a two-door beauty I loved. Country music filled the car as we jammed along, creating a bubble of happiness that I wished could last forever. But as we pulled into a familiar neighborhood and came to a stop, I recognized that we were at Dad's place.

"Hey, I know this place," I remember thinking, my stomach dropping in anticipation. My Mom didn't communicate with me earlier that she was going to drop me off at my father's house, and I was supposed to stay there for some time. Even later, my parents never told me when they would drop me off at the other's place, so a shadow of uncertainty hung over me.

When we got to my Dad's house, he was waiting for me and came to the car, telling me it was time to come out. Confusion gripped me, and I looked at Mom for affirmation. *Why was I here? Why was my Mom not getting out of the car? Was I supposed to stay at Dad's house without her?*

All those questions swirled in my head, and my body froze momentarily. As the reality sunk in that my mother was leaving me with Dad, I immediately started bawling. I didn't want to leave Mom as she was all that I had known in those three years after my parents' divorce.

But she assured me, saying, "It's okay, I'll be back in a couple of days. You're gonna have a good time with your Dad."

Despite her comforting words, I couldn't move. Tears welled up in my eyes as I pleaded, "Mom, I don't wanna go. I don't wanna leave you."

The next thing I knew, I was on my Dad's front lawn, my eyes still glued to my Mom in the car. She was still telling me that I had to go, but tears streaked her face as well, knowing that I was in pain at having to be separated from her.

She couldn't take the pain of it all and drove away, but her tear-stained face and the retreating Thunderbird were etched in my memory for a long time. The pain of leaving one parent to go with the other was almost unbearable. I knew I was not alone, as every child of divorced parents must have felt this pain at some point or other. But at that moment, I felt truly isolated in my anguish.

As I grew older, the challenges of living in two separate households became more apparent. Life at my Dad's place was very different from the normal I was used to at my mother's place. Staying with my Dad, I was the middle child of four siblings—an older brother, a younger brother, and a younger sister—with a new stepmom. I felt constantly overlooked, caught in the middle child syndrome. My older brother was the all-star athlete, my younger brother was the baby of the family, and my sister was the only girl. Where did I fit in?

This lack of attention bred feelings of neglect and low self-esteem. I struggled to find my identity, often feeling like I had to compete with either my older or younger brother to get the love and attention I craved. Sometimes, it felt that as the middle child, I had no role in my Dad's family.

My older brother was the trailblazer and the apple of my father's eye. He was the best in every sport, be it BMX racing, golf, or football. I idolized him so much because I saw how proud Dad was of him and wanted him to feel the same way toward me, but I never got the attention my brother could easily receive.

Then, my younger siblings were adored because they were the babies of the family. But I was just Jack, the second son, who tried his best to match up with his siblings but couldn't. Balanced precariously between my siblings, I felt that if I needed my Dad's attention, I couldn't be myself—I had to be better like my elder brother or more adorable like my younger siblings.

That feeling of never being enough and always feeling competition between my siblings and me built conflict between us. Of course, I didn't hate them, but I was jealous. As a six-year-old struggling to find my place and role in the new family I was left with, I was just desperate for acknowledgment. It was during these moments that I began to build what I now recognize as mental resilience, though at the time, it felt more like survival.

I learned at a young age that while living in my Dad's house, I needed to seek my own attention and learn how to make my own change through friends or other sources where I could find acknowledgment. In retrospect, I realize this environment forced me to develop independence and peacemaking abilities. But it also taught me to suppress my emotions, a coping mechanism that would have long-lasting effects.

Life at my mom's house was a stark contrast. There, I was often alone as my older brother chose to spend more time with my Dad as he got older. Thus, I was an only child with my Mom and the sole object of all her attention. However, my mother's financial state was different from my father's, and the stress of making ends meet was evident, even in my young eyes.

My mom, a hardworking woman who sacrificed everything for us, did her best to provide the best life she could manage. She worked two jobs, cleaning houses to make ends meet. I am forever grateful for my mother's sacrifices to help me become the person I am today. Her unwavering support and guidance have had a profound and lasting impact on my life.

When I was twelve, we moved into a trailer park, which brought its own set of challenges. I was just becoming my own person, facing life head-on. I couldn't help but think about the start of the contrast between my mother's and father's lives. My Dad was living the good life as he had a family, his second wife, three children aside from me, and a Pine Valley golf course membership. I resented him and his lifestyle because while he was living well, my Mom and I had to move into that trailer park.

I attended school in my Dad's more affluent neighborhood, which led to social stigma and bullying as the rest of my peers viewed me as a boy from the trailer park. The students bullied me and used to mention that my Mom cleaned houses and I lived in a trailer.

Aside from that stigma, the limited opportunities and exposure to a volatile environment in the trailer park added another layer of complexity to my upbringing. It wasn't uncommon to randomly hear a couple fighting or the cops being called two or three trailers down. To me, it was normal because it was the environment I was growing up in while I was staying with Mom. It was a part of life in a trailer park.

When I look back on those days spent with my mother, I see that it created parental stress for her. Now that I am a parent myself, I realize how difficult it must have been for her back then. With the small income she earned from her two jobs, I can't even imagine how she managed to provide for us.

Aside from these memories of a boy with divorced parents, I can't forget the time my childhood changed forever. Nothing could have prepared me for my 13th birthday—a day that lives rent-free in my mind. I have sought help through therapy and discussions with others to address how I felt. But the guilt and sadness about how that particular day turned out stays with me to this day.

While I love my parents deeply and will always care for them, I now understand that no one is perfect, and even the most heroic figures in our lives—our parents—are human and make mistakes. As a child, it is easy to see our parents as flawless and invincible, but adulthood provides a better understanding of the challenges they face.

On my thirteenth birthday, Dad had promised to take me to a Fort Wayne Komets hockey game, just the two of us. I spent the entire day at school bursting with excitement, my mind racing with thoughts of finally having quality time with my father. It felt like I had been waiting for that moment my whole life.

After school, I rushed home, donned my favorite hockey jersey, and sat on the curb in front of our trailer, waiting with all the anticipation a boy who had just turned thirteen could muster. I was excited that I would get to spend the best day of my life. But fate had other plans. My eyes focused on every car coming into the vicinity. *Is that my Dad's car?* The question lingered in the air, but a long time passed, and I didn't see his car as I had hoped.

As the minutes ticked by and the sun began to set, my excitement slowly turned to confusion and crushing disappointment. Dad never came. I sat out on the curb, still waiting, until it was too dark to see the road and spot his car. Mom watched silently from the porch, likely at a loss for words. I remember feeling my heart shatter in slow motion. To this day, I can picture every second of that night.

It wasn't just a missed game—it was the moment I realized that perhaps I wasn't as special as I had thought. A part of me stayed on that curb that night, forever waiting for a father who would never show up. That night was the start of a very long road that would shape me for the rest of my life.

The next day, nursing the wounds of my first real heartbreak, I made a decision I would regret for the rest of my life. I called my dad on our old landline phone, and I couldn't contain my emotions when he answered. I screamed, cried, and poured out all my anger and sadness. In a moment of unfiltered pain, I told him I never wanted to see him again.

Those words cut deep, and my dad took them to heart. I didn't see him for three years after that. At that time, I felt I had finally gotten rid of the person due to whom my life was in shambles. Perhaps I just needed someone to blame, and I put it all on my father, making myself believe that I would be better off without him.

The years after that blowout with Dad were a mixture of highs and lows, with my mom trying to be both parents for me while juggling two jobs. I often found myself alone, navigating adolescence without a father figure to guide me.

The void left by my father's absence and my older brother's choice to live with him was one I tried to fill in various ways, some healthier than others. In many ways, that 13-year-old boy is still on that curb, waiting for his father. But that moment was also the catalyst for my journey of self-reliance and resilience.

Each hardship and struggle I endured contributed to the person I have become. The lack of stability and the constant need to adapt taught me resilience and resourcefulness. The emotional turbulence of my early years made me more empathetic and better able to understand and relate to the struggles of others.

Living in a financially constrained household also instilled a profound appreciation for the little things. I learned to find joy in small victories and cherish moments of peace and happiness amidst the chaos.

Without those early struggles, I might not have developed the same level of determination and perseverance. In reflection, I see that my childhood, though far from ideal, was a crucible that forged my character.

Now that I am a father myself, I know I'm far from perfect as a parent, but I have learned that being present matters more than anything else. I make sure my son knows he is special and loved and will never be the boy sitting on the curb with a broken heart.

The scars from my childhood have become the foundation of my strength as a father, reminding me every day of the power of showing up for those we love. These scars remind me of what I have overcome and prove my resilience. They testify that our past, no matter how difficult, can be a powerful catalyst for growth and self-discovery.

Chapter 3: Leaving on an Airplane

"The soldier, above all others, prays for peace, for it is the soldier who must suffer and bear the deepest wounds and scars of war."

—Douglas MacArthur

Sometimes, I wonder if I would be the same person I am today if I hadn't joined the military.

Would I still be the resilient warrior after my life experiences as a soldier, or would I be someone entirely different?

The answer to this question eludes me.

My time in the military is unforgettable as it broke me down entirely, brought me to my lowest points during training, and then made me face the toughest state man has to go through—war. The dreams I had for my future were very different from what I chose, but if I hadn't set out on this career path, I would not have been the same.

I had always wanted to be a teacher. Gaining knowledge and then imparting it to others has been my passion from a very early age. Giving to others has always brought me great joy, and I wanted it to be a big part of my profession.

During my senior year of high school, I took a program in which I had to go to high school for half a day the whole year and then teach at an elementary school in the second half. I could have graduated early, but I indulged in my passion and taught children. Thus, when I finally graduated high school, I wanted to pursue teaching. However, as I lived with my mother and we did not have enough money to gain a higher education, I knew I didn't have a lot of career options.

However, my mother suggested that I join the military, and she told me about the Air Force National Guard. Shortly after, I met with a recruiter who told me that if I joined, they would pay for my college, and I would get to travel the world. They even promised to pay an extra $800 monthly to go to college. I felt like it was a pretty good deal for joining the military. I was also told that I would only have to work one weekend a month and then for two weeks annually. It sounded too good to be true.

However, the recruiter didn't tell me about the possibility of being deployed overseas and fighting a war. So, ignoring that side of the picture, I signed my name that day. It was the 13th of June, 2007, a day that changed my life. They gave me $15,000 as a signing bonus, and back then, I felt I had made the right decision. So, I joined the Air Force and had to leave for basic training in January 2008.

At that time, I was nineteen and thought I was doing the right thing for myself and my mom. Like every other nineteen-year-old, I thought I knew everything and could take on any challenge. Two days before I had to leave for basic training, the weight of my decisions settled in, and it hit me that I was actually leaving. It was like leaving a part of my life behind, the world I knew, to step into an unknown world full of dangers and unfamiliar faces.

It was overwhelming, to say the very least.

I was not taking anything except my backpack, and it hit me all at once. Was I making the right choice? I was going to join the military, and for those two days, the worries settled in and held me in a chokehold.

Nevertheless, the decisions were made, and there was no escape route. I chose it for myself and knew I had to get through like the resilient warrior I prided myself on being. I was sent to Texas for basic training via airplane. After landing, I waited for two hours, and then about forty or fifty more guys showed up. Then we got on a bus to take us to Lackland Air Force Base in San Antonio, Texas. It was the place where our basic training had to commence.

After a two-hour ride, we reached the base, and the training instructor came up to the bus. He had a flat hat that barely covered his eyes, and he yelled so loud that it startled me. He ordered all of us to get off the lineup, and all fifty of us ran off the bus lineup.

It was cold, and I tried to put my coat on, but in my hurry, I didn't notice that it was inside out. I realized that if it is your first week and you do something like that in front of a training instructor, they will ridicule you and break you down. It is their job to tear down everything you have learned from society until you are at your lowest, and they build you back up with their core foundations and values.

So I had put my jacket on inside out, and the training instructor got just an inch away from my face and yelled, "Are you retarded, boy? Take your jacket off and put it on the right way."

I was not used to being yelled at, but he was right there in my face, yelling at the top of his lungs. It was shocking, and all I could think was that it would be seven long weeks of training.

I was right in thinking that. It was a long seven weeks and an absolute hell for us to endure. In the basic training, their motto is to break you down and make you mentally weak and scared. So you don't get enough sleep, barely five hours a night, and you are constantly being yelled at. In such a hostile environment, the only thing you can do is rely on the other soldiers for help and comfort.

Later on, I realized this was called trauma bonding and was the main reason why people in the military were such good soldiers. So we learned to rely on the fifty people in our unit who were going through the same struggles, and all of us helped each other get through the training. I made lifelong friends there and still talk to them even though years have passed since our basic training. But the bonds we made back then were strong, and we all remember each other as our support and motivation to keep going.

In our unit, we were all assigned different jobs. Some people had to keep the chrome on all the doors shiny using toothbrushes, and some had to make sure all the beds were made correctly. I was the laundry king, basically in charge of doing the laundry with three other guys who helped me. So we were in charge of making sure all fifty troops had clean laundry each day.

I remember the little comments we made when we brought the laundry back. "For the last time, you guys. Quit pooping in your underwear!" So I would say that as I tossed each troop their clothes. All those little banter and arguments were a respite from all the screaming and yelling we had to endure. So we lived off of those little moments because we knew we would have a lot to face during the training sessions.

In the second week of training, none of us were sleeping, and we were all very irritated. We had about twenty-five bunk beds in a room that was 200 feet by 50 feet, and we were packed in tight. So, one night, the guy next to me was snoring, and the loud noise kept me from sleeping. I was worn out and needed to close my eyes, but his snores kept irritating me.

I tried to wake him up, saying, "Hey man, you are snoring."

It didn't go as planned because instead of stopping the snores, it only made him mad at me. He woke up and punched me in the face. Hearing the commotion, everyone in the unit was focused on us.

One of the guys said, "My, my, it's the middle of the night. You are not supposed to make any noise."

However, it made his anger worse, and he started punching again. By then, I was hit three times and in the middle of a full-blown fight at one in the morning just because I woke a kid up.

I put him in a headlock and choked him down to the ground, saying, "Are we done? Are we done?"

It felt like we had jumped over three different beds and hit each other so many times. But it was one of my first real fights, and after that fight, we never had an issue again. I didn't hear that guy snore, either. I don't know if he never went to sleep for the remaining five weeks, but we were cool with each other after that.

But it shows how on edge we all were during training, as just being woken up resulted in an actual fistfight. While we were at the base, we eventually got used to the rough conditions and all the yelling. It became our normal, and it didn't faze us anymore like it used to when we had just come to Texas.

However, the hardest part for me was the meals because we had only five minutes for each meal. So we got to eat for only fifteen minutes a day. We had to stand in a buffet-like line to get our food, and we were starving and dying of thirst due to all the training. But we didn't have enough time to eat anything, so I learned how to eat fast and basically wolf down my food because I wouldn't get anything otherwise. It was the hardest part for me because I loved food so much. Even now, whenever I am anxious, I can eat a whole meal in just one minute, and my family is shocked to see this. I only tell them that if they went to basic training for the military, they would understand.

Another thing that I had to get accustomed to in training was staying away from my family. It was also very hard because I was taken away from the people I loved, living in a remote place that was miles away from home. Then, we couldn't contact our families as frequently as we wanted to. And when we were finally allowed to call home after two and a half weeks of training, we were given only three minutes each.

There were six payphones set up outside our dorms, and we took turns to go and make our calls, tell the family our address, and say that we were safe, then hang up. So I waited in line, convincing myself I wouldn't cry. I was mentally resilient and strong enough not to cry over a phone call.

However, when it was my turn, I called my mom, and as soon as she picked up and said hello, all the emotions hit me with full force. I said, "Mom, it's me." And the rest of the words were incoherent as we were both crying.

She was at Walmart, and there was a lot of noise around her, so she told everyone to shut up. The time was running out, so I could barely manage to give her my address so she could send mail. In tears, I told her that I was doing alright. Hearing her voice after so long made me realize how much I valued her and missed her. So that was one more thing I learned from the basic training: the importance of family. After those three minutes, I had to return to the drill.

Three and half weeks later, we would get a mail call every other day. We were allowed to go to a break room, and our drill sergeant would bring all fifty of us into the room. We would sit in formation, and he would pick up a big bin with all our mail. Then he toppled it upside down, emptying it of its contents.

So we all sat there, waiting for our names to be called so we could get our mail. But the drill sergeant read the first three letters out to everyone. The letter he read, a trainee's girlfriend had sent her pictures with that letter, and the sergeant showed them to everyone, making a fuss about it. I looked at the guy whose letter he was reading, and he was all red in the face because of embarrassment.

But none of us could protest against it because if we did, he would make us do the worst duties available and set us up for running and push-ups. So the first three letters were read out, and then he called my name. My heart started racing when I finally got a letter. But then, knowing he would read it out loud made that excitement falter.

"Oh, it's from your mommy, huh?" He exclaimed and, much to my surprise, added, "I'm not going to read this."

I let out a sigh of relief, but it was too soon. He looked down at the bottom and found a piece of fur in that letter. My mom sent some fur from my border collie Zippy, who I have had since I was thirteen. She cut some fur off my dog and taped it to my letter, probably as a sign of reassurance. I was shocked. Why would she do that? It was worse because the drill sergeant showed it to everyone. I felt quite embarrassed back then. I had never been laughed at so hard by all the other forty-nine guys from my unit. But it became a memory I held close after the training; all my unit laughed at me because my mom sent me some fur to make me feel better.

Seven weeks later, as my basic training was completed, I graduated top of the class. I received the Honor Graduate award for scoring highest on the written test and performing the best on the physical test, and all the recognition made me think I was doing well in the Air Force. Then, I was sent to tech school for four and a half months, during which I had to learn how to do my job in the Air Force. I went to Northern Texas at the Shepherd Air Force Base, where I learned to be a weapons aircraft mechanic. I trained and became a weapons specialist on F-16.

Thus, I finally returned home after six months of staying away from my family. I thought nothing would have changed back home in my absence, but I found out that everything had changed when I got there. My friends and family had gotten used to me not being there with them, so I had to start over. It was almost hard for me to leave my military friends, too, because we had bonded so well together, and they were a part of my daily life that I left behind when I came home.

It was hard to adjust on both sides. I wanted to hang out with my friends and family, but they were often busy. I was twenty back then and thought, why didn't anyone want to hang out with me anymore? I was selfish and wanted their attention, but they had their own lives and affairs to tend to. So, I decided to take advantage of my free college degree.

I enrolled in Purdue University Fort Wayne in Indiana and started pursuing a secondary education. I wanted to be a math teacher, so I took the degree program and invested time and effort into it. So I was going to college, working one week a month for the Air Force, and I had a job at Lowe's. I was trying hard to excel in my studies and live the life I wanted to. A year and a half passed as such.

However, I realized that college was great, but the starting salary for a teacher back in 2009 was just $40,000. I was working hard to get a degree only to find a job that paid forty grand. I felt that all my time and investment was being wasted. At that time, my father offered me to work at a steel company with him called Steel Dynamics. There, I started off with a salary of $70,000.

So, I was twenty-two years old when I dropped out of college and started working at that steel company with my father. It was the year 2010, and I learned some extreme life lessons about what it was like to work hard in tough conditions. I was working four to six days a week on 12-hour shifts. I did that job for six and a half years, and we had to switch schedules, working day shifts for a few days and then switching to night shifts.

The time I worked in the steel company was also when I reworked my relationship with my father. He worked about a hundred yards away from me as the steel plant was huge. So whenever I took a break, I would go to him and hang out.

Those six to seven years of my working with him helped rekindle our friendship, and we got really close.

We would go out and have beers and wings every other week or so. I worked with him, and it was fun despite all the hard work. I was making good money, and it felt like my life was all sorted out. About six to seven years had passed since my enlistment, and everything was on the right track for me.

I was twenty-five then but had not been in a serious relationship. I would just date and move on because I felt like I had other things to care about. I wanted to travel the world and spend time with my friends and family, so dating wasn't a priority until twenty-five. But then, I met a girl who changed my perspective.

I met her in 2013, and she became the first woman I truly fell in love with. She was everything I could have wanted in a partner, so after just one year of going out, I was deeply in love and wanted to spend the rest of my life with her. But then, fate struck, and in October 2014, I was deployed to Afghanistan for the first time.

I hadn't yet started a family of my own, but leaving everyone behind with little chance of returning was tough. I had never been to war before, but I had heard stories that made me think about whether I would face all the cruelty firsthand. So I trained myself to focus on the fact that about 300 of my comrades were going with me; I was not alone, and I would make it through no matter what happened.

Afghanistan was my first encounter with war and being at the frontline in battle. Our job was to provide close air support for the army and marine infantry. So our A-10 had to fly very low, and we would bomb and shoot the opposing side's soldiers. If you ever talk to any army or marine guy about an A-10, they will tell you that it's the best aircraft and has saved them many times.

So we were deployed with an A-10, left for Germany, and then flew into Qatar, where we had to stay for five days. In Qatar, we were allowed to drink three beers a day. We even had a pool and a movie theater. So, I was confused for the first five days because it didn't feel like war but a vacation. Little did I know that the real war was about to start.

Five days later, we were put on a C-130, a cargo plane that was going to transfer us. We had our body armor and helmet on and also had a big bag that had all our essentials. We were also given an M16A1 with a gun that we had to carry with us at all times. So, we were on board the C-130, which was a giant tube, and we were sitting there sideways. It almost felt like we were packed in like sardines.

It was a two-hour flight to the Bagram Air Base in Afghanistan, which was surrounded by mountains. So we had to do a combat landing there as the ISIS and the Taliban could shoot at us from the mountain ranges. It was the first time I had been part of a combat landing, and it felt like a wild roller coaster with no idea where we were headed.

That landing was my first realization that we were at war. For the first twenty-four hours, we couldn't sleep, but later on, on our first shift, I saw the place where I was supposed to sleep, and I slept only for five hours. Then it was back to war with no knowing whether we would make it out alive or not.

As I was putting all my equipment away on my first shift, I heard a siren go off. If you ask any soldier about the siren, they will tell you that it was an ultimate call to action. The alarm meant we were getting attacked, and we had to hit the ground and find cover immediately. It was the first time I got mortared, and for a second, my body froze, but then I sprang into action with the realization that I was in Afghanistan and I had to do my duty.

From then onward, it was a regular situation to be mortared by the enemy. We would be eating food, and a mortar attack would happen; it was almost becoming normal for us. Two weeks later, I got a letter from my girlfriend, and I found it odd because she could have just called me because we had phones and WiFi at the base. Instead, she sent me a letter telling me that she was breaking up with me. So, imagine this: I am at war in Afghanistan, I am in a constant combat situation, and I get this letter from the love of my life saying that she can no longer be with me.

I felt heartbroken, but I had no time to cry. War really leaves you with no time on your hands. So it was a terrible feeling in my heart but a constant urgency in my head because I was at war. I couldn't concentrate properly, but I knew I had to survive and do my job.

After about thirty-one days in Afghanistan, the Air Force told us that we needed to pack up and go to Kuwait. So, my unit became one of the first to go and destroy ISIS's personnel and equipment in Kuwait. For five months, we stayed at a Marine base in Kuwait and fought with ISIS. I felt like I was finally doing God's work by getting rid of evil people who were involved in so many crimes, human trafficking, and murdering innocent civilians.

Another wild memory I have from Kuwait is when we encountered a sandstorm. It was like a massive wall of sand that covered half of the sky and moved so fast that it hurt. The sky had changed colors from blue to orangish yellow as that sandstorm engulfed us. It was something I had never experienced before.

However, my first deployment was a series of events that tested my mental resilience. We shared a tent with ten other people for five months. We had a small air conditioning unit and bunk beds. We also had to walk a quarter mile to go to the toilet or to take a shower. It was a tough time, but we made it through.

By April 2015, I had returned home, and it felt as though nothing would ever be the same again. The experience of fighting in the war had left me with PTSD, and even the slightest trigger could send me into a state of fight or flight. The military excels at training us for combat and preparing us to face the horrors of the battlefield, but they fall short when it comes to helping us reintegrate into a normal and peaceful life. We soldiers are trained to be resilient and strong, yet the emotional and psychological scars we carry are often overlooked.

Coming back home, I found myself in a world that was both familiar and alien. The daily routines and simple pleasures that once brought me comfort now seemed distant and unreachable. Ordinary sounds, like a car backfiring or fireworks, would set off a cascade of memories, plunging me back into the chaos of war. Nightmares plagued my sleep, and the hyper-vigilance that had kept me alive on the battlefield made it difficult to relax or feel safe.

The support systems available were inadequate, leaving many of us to navigate our trauma on our own. Therapy and counseling were often hard to access, and the stigma surrounding mental health issues in the military community made it difficult to seek help. We were expected to be tough, to push through, and to carry on as if nothing had changed. But everything had changed. The war had altered our perception of the world and ourselves in ways that were profound and irrevocable. The camaraderie and brotherhood that had sustained us in the field were replaced by isolation and a sense of disconnect upon returning home. Friends and family, despite their best intentions, could not fully understand the depth of our experiences.

The military might prepare us for war, but it does little to prepare us for the peace that follows. We are left to grapple with our trauma, often feeling abandoned and alone, as we attempt to find a new normal in a world that no longer feels familiar.

Chapter 4: The Battle of Custody

"We all grow up. Hopefully, we get wiser. Age brings wisdom, and fatherhood changes one's life completely."

—Frank Abagnale

After I returned from my first deployment, I was still recuperating from the aftermath of war and the trauma it left me with. It had not been more than two or three weeks since I returned home that my friends invited me to a baseball game to cheer me up. They wanted me to relax and enjoy my life again, soaking in the reality that I was no longer on the battlefield.

However, that baseball game changed the course of my life, and it became the reason I met the woman who became the mother of my only child. I met her at the game, and we instantly connected due to our similar habits of being adrenaline junkies and having an independent mindset. We started dating, but two months into our relationship, we found out that she was pregnant with my child.

Hearing the news that I was about to become a father was both exciting and overwhelming at the same time. I remember the exact moment—my partner's eyes filled with a mix of joy and apprehension as she shared the news. While a part of me was thrilled at the prospect of bringing a new life into the world, another part of me was paralyzed by fear. I had just returned from the war, and the scars, both visible and invisible, were still fresh.

Every night, I grappled with nightmares and flashbacks, reliving the harrowing experiences on the battlefield. The mental space I found myself in was dark and turbulent, and the idea of having the responsibility of a young soul when I was still trying to heal from my traumas felt incredibly daunting. I questioned my ability to be a good father and to provide the love and stability that a child deserves. The switch from living with my traumas to suddenly preparing for fatherhood was abrupt and jarring. I realized that I had to shift my focus from my own pain to the needs of my unborn child. This realization was both a burden and a beacon of hope. It forced me to confront my struggles head-on, seek help, and start the long journey toward healing with renewed determination.

There were days when the weight of it all seemed unbearable, but the thought of my child kept me going. I imagined holding my baby for the first time, seeing their tiny fingers wrap around mine, and hearing their first cries. These images became my anchor, giving me the strength to navigate through my darkest moments. In time, I learned to balance my healing process with the preparations for fatherhood. I attended therapy sessions, joined support groups, and gradually started to feel a sense of hope and purpose.

The road was not easy, but knowing that I had a child on the way gave me the motivation to keep moving forward. The anticipation of fatherhood became a powerful catalyst for my recovery, transforming my fears into a deep resolve to be the best father I could be.

I wasn't sure if I was doing alright myself, but I wanted to give my child everything he needed or wanted from me. In short, I wished to be the best dad and fully play my part. It was nothing short of overwhelming for a man who had just returned from war and was still adjusting to normal human society. Every day felt like a battle of a different kind—one that required emotional resilience and a strength I wasn't sure I possessed.

Returning from war had left me feeling disconnected from the world I once knew. Simple tasks seemed daunting, and social interactions were often fraught with anxiety. The cacophony of civilian life felt alien after the structured chaos of the battlefield. I was still learning to reintegrate, to find my place in a society that moved on while I was away. My mind was a battleground of its own, filled with the echoes of gunfire and the cries of my fallen comrades.

Yet, amidst this turmoil, the thought of my child became a guiding light. I envisioned the milestones we would share—the first steps, the first words, the countless bedtime stories. I wanted to be there for all of it, to be a constant source of love and support. I wanted to ensure that my child would never feel the absence of a caring father, even if it meant confronting my own demons head-on. I started by setting small, manageable goals for myself. Each day, I worked on creating a stable environment, both physically and emotionally.

I reached out to fellow veterans who had successfully navigated the transition to fatherhood, seeking their advice and drawing strength from their experiences. Their stories of resilience and hope reassured me that it was possible to heal and thrive as a parent.

There were setbacks and moments of doubt, times when the weight of my past threatened to overwhelm me. But each time, I reminded myself of the promise I made—to be the best dad I could be. Slowly, the fog of war began to lift, replaced by the clarity of my new purpose. Preparing for fatherhood became a journey of healing and transformation. I found joy in the simple acts of assembling the crib, choosing baby clothes, and reading parenting books.

These tasks, though mundane to some, were monumental to me. They signified a new chapter, a new beginning where I was not just a survivor but a father ready to give his all. In embracing my role as a father, I found a renewed sense of hope and strength. I realized that while I couldn't change the past, I had the power to shape the future—for myself and for my child. This realization gave me the courage to face each day with a sense of purpose and a heart full of love. It was a challenging path, but one that I was determined to walk, hand in hand with my child, towards a brighter tomorrow.

Despite the unknown challenges that lay ahead of me, I thought I would brace myself and get through this for my child. I had to be the perfect father and provide my children with everything I couldn't have in my childhood. Growing up in two separate homes with parents who were no longer together made me feel that I had to do everything possible to give my child a complete family and lots of happy memories. Sadly, that wish could not come to fruition.

My girlfriend and I couldn't carry our relationship forward despite the pregnancy. Thus, in the third month of dating each other, we ended our relationship. Our perspectives on life were different, and so were our personalities. In those three months, we had figured out that we couldn't work as a couple in the long run and were better off apart.

I took the mother of my child to the hospital, stayed with her for the twelve long hours that she was in labor, and got to see my son come into the world. Holding my child in my arms felt like I had conquered every war in the world, and my life didn't belong to me anymore. Instead, it was all dedicated to him.

While it was amazing to hold my son and accept that I had become a father at twenty-seven, it was painful to be told shortly after that, for the first six months, I would only get to see my boy twice a week for three hours. I wanted to be with him in every moment and milestone of his life, but as his custody was given to his mother, I had to abide by the minimum visitation rights.

It was hell for me because I had just become a father, and I was excited to be with my son, but the court's decision took that away from me. I couldn't experience all the little moments with him as much as I wanted. His first attempts to crawl, his first steps, and his first words were milestones I couldn't see unfolding in front of me.

Even though fatherhood came to me, I couldn't experience it fully due to the custody restraints put on me by the court system in Indiana. I had thought of so many things that I wished to do with my boy but couldn't get the opportunity. Since I have always been athletic, I had thought of being a football coach to my son. I had imagined what it would be like to teach him to be strong and fast and to play catch with him every day. Unfortunately, given the scarce visitation hours I had with my son on court orders, those wishes could not take a step from imagination to reality.

I wanted to be there for her and my child, but our decision to no longer be in a relationship put us in a tough spot with the judicial system of Indiana. In some states of the US, the law for child custody when parents are no longer married or together is 50-50 custody. However, in Indiana, custody immediately goes to the mother in case of divorce or single parents. The father is allowed only two three-hour visits per month with the child.

A stereotype has formed in society about men having children with women they are no longer together with, which gives them a bad reputation. Mostly, people believe they didn't want to take the responsibility and custody of their child, so they left the baby with the mother and got off by only paying child support. However, that is not entirely true for all men. Some of us want to take responsibility and share happy memories with our children but are stripped of the possibility through legal constraints.

I know there are a lot of men out there who want to be with their children, spend time with them, and be a part of their lives more than the courts and the mother of their child wants them to. So, they have to fight through the system just to be allowed enough time with their child, putting in their money, effort, and time to keep going to court to get their rights acknowledged.

In a nutshell, it is quite painful, and it tests your mental resilience. Going through a situation similar to mine, where I was still coping with PTSD and depression, then at the same time fighting for more time with my son, requires a lot of mental resilience and patience.

When my son, Jaxon, was born, I was working four days a week. Normally, I worked six days a week and got two days off. Thinking about the future and all the time I should give to my son and his mother, I quit my job at the SDI and started working as a CVS manager. Thus, I got a job with comparatively fewer working hours so that I could spend sufficient time with my family.

For the first six months, I had to stick to the three-hour visits a week with my child. But after six months, I was able to get a court date that would decide my future with my son. My child's mother lived in Fort Wayne, Indiana, but she decided to move an hour and a half south of Indianapolis. I got the notification, and my first thought was that she was taking my kid away.

I remember my lawyer telling me that I was going to lose in court. I fired him the next day because how could he say that when I was paying him to fight for my case? I had just paid him $2500 that week, yet he had the audacity to tell me that I would lose in court and, therefore, settle my case in mediation.

But I paid no heed to his words. I got a new lawyer, and I went to court for Jaxon, appealing my case to the judge. However, I was only given minimum visitation rights. I could keep Jaxon with me overnight and pay three four-hour visits to him per month. It wasn't as much as I wanted, but considerably better than the previous arrangement.

It felt like a step in the right direction for me for some time, and I became assured that I was slowly working toward my goal. However, as she had moved so far away, I had to drive all the way there and back just to spend some time with my boy. Then, as she had to come to get him from my place, she would tell me to drop him off as it was too far for her. I agreed as I wanted to be on good terms with her and keep seeing Jackson, but deep down, I thought it was unfair. She decided to move so far and wanted to keep Jackson away from me. Why was I putting up with the aftermath of her decisions?

But I gave in due to my son and my desire to see him often. Two years had passed since Jaxon's birth, and I realized that battling for his custody in court would lead me nowhere. So, I was advised to settle it out of court, and I ended up offering his mother $5,000 cash at mediation just to convince her to let me spend a weekend and a night with my boy. She agreed, and the arrangement continued as I kept paying her for about two and a half years until I was deployed again. By then, I had already put $20,000 into the court system through lawyers and a Guardian ad Litem, a lawyer who represented Jackson. It cost money to keep the case going, and every phone call amounted to $300.

It was a tough time for me, and I felt the court system was designed to obtain as much money as possible from both parties. The lawyers, judges, paralegals, and Guardian ad Litem were all means of getting the clients to spend more money and invest more time into the case. For the last seven or eight years, the mother of my child and I have spent over $90,000 in court fees altogether, which is terrible because it was all due to the fact that we didn't agree on who should get to see Jaxon more and spend time with him.

Sometimes, I wish I could call our senator in Indiana and ask him to change the law about child custody to 50-50. Many fathers out there want to be a part of their children's lives but can't because this law of child custody is weighted more in favor of the mother.

In hindsight, it's absolutely silly how our case went down, and I know we would both want to go back and change it if we could. But back then, we were both so passionate about our standpoints that we couldn't back off. Thus, our case became a string of court dates, lawyers, court fees, and more with no plausible outcome. She didn't back off because she wanted to keep the custody and the child care support. And I didn't let go because I wanted to be a permanent part of my son's life, not just a figure who existed only to pay for his expenses.

On the day he was born, I vowed to be with him and watch him grow into a young, handsome, and successful man. I had promised to make happy memories with my boy. So, I couldn't give up the fight either.

I could no longer work as a CVS manager as I didn't have time to focus on my job and then take long hours off to drive to and from Indianapolis. So, I left that job and reached out to one of my comrades from the military, asking him if I could get a job at the base. He connected me with my boss, who gave me a temporary position for three months, saying they would hire me if I did well enough.

With that new job, I had the weekend and every Monday off. So I could drive to Indianapolis every Monday and see my son. Things worked out, and I could keep Jaxon with me for the three nights that I had off. I didn't have a full-time job, but I was making the best of what I had. It was tough juggling my working hours, the long drives to Indianapolis, and spending time with Jaxon, but I did it out of love for my boy.

I still resent the court system for not recognizing that I deserved to be with my son. I was a good father, devoted and loving, but for some reason, I was unfairly portrayed as a man who didn't care. This misrepresentation was likely fueled by the pervasive stereotype about single fathers—that most of them are uninterested in or incapable of properly caring for their children.

However, I was not like them. I yearned to be an integral part of my son's life, to watch him grow, and to guide him through life's challenges and joys. Every moment spent with him was precious to me. I cherished the times we laughed together, the bedtime stories, and even the small, everyday moments that make up the fabric of a child's life. I wanted to be there for his first day of school, to help with his homework, to teach him how to ride a bike, and to celebrate his achievements, no matter how small.

When I looked at my son, I saw a future filled with shared experiences and mutual growth. I imagined taking him to the park, coaching his little league team, and having heart-to-heart talks as he navigated the ups and downs of growing up. My love for him was profound and unwavering, and I was determined to be the best father I could be.

The court system failed to see this. They seemed to focus on outdated stereotypes rather than the reality of my commitment and dedication. I was painted with the same broad brush as fathers who may have been absent or negligent, but I was neither. Instead, I was a father who wanted nothing more than to be there for his son, to support and nurture him in every way possible. The pain of being separated from my son, of not being able to fulfill my role as his father, was immense. It felt as though a part of my heart was being torn away.

The court's decision did not just affect me; it affected my son as well. He was deprived of a father who loved him deeply and wanted to be a constant presence in his life. To this day, the injustice of that decision lingers in my mind, a constant reminder of the prejudice and misunderstanding that can permeate the legal system. Despite this, my love for my son remains undiminished, and I continue to hope for a future where I can be the father he deserves.

The mother of my child was dating other men, and while I didn't want anything to do with her personal life, I needed her to acknowledge that I could be a good parent to Jaxon. She had to stop ripping me of the right to see my boy grow up and raise him.

The day my son was born, it felt as if I had been reborn too. I vividly recall holding him in my arms and thinking that my life revolved completely around him. Before his birth, I had only ever thought about myself, and my life focused on me. But after I held him and looked at the boy who shared my flesh and blood, I knew that I could go to hell and back for him. I could do anything to see his smile and lay the whole world at his feet if it made him happy. That day, I understood what it felt like to be a father. Thus, accepting fatherhood changed me completely.

Sometimes, my family would ask me if I would rather be the hero or the villain. It is a harmless question with a simple response, and most people choose to be the hero. When I think about it, the hero would sacrifice 10,000 people to save millions. But I am the sort of person who would sacrifice millions of people to save that one person close to my heart—my son. So, thinking in those terms, I feel I would rather be a villain who does everything possible to keep that one cherished person safe. That just goes on to show how dedicated I am to my son and how his well-being was my foremost priority.

I fought in a war, facing the harsh realities and life-threatening dangers on the battlefield. The experience was grueling, testing every ounce of my courage and strength. When the war ended, a new kind of battle began—one fought not with weapons but with words and legal arguments in the courtroom. This fight was for something far more precious to me: the right to be a considerable part of my son's life. All I ever wanted was for my boy to be happy and to grow up knowing his father loved him deeply. The legal system, with its complexities and often slow-moving processes, was another formidable opponent.

There were moments when the struggle seemed insurmountable, and I felt on the verge of exhaustion. But the mental resilience I had built up over the years, shaped by the rigors of military service, kept me going. Each setback in the courtroom only strengthened my resolve. The vision of my son, the thought of his laughter and his dreams, was my beacon of hope. I imagined him at the end of the finish line, cheering me on. This image fueled my determination, giving me the strength to push through every obstacle. Knowing I had a child gave my life a new sense of purpose and ambition. It was no longer just about me; it was about building a future where my son could thrive and feel secure in the love of his father.

Despite the emotional and physical toll, I kept fighting. Each legal document filed, each court appearance, and each argument made was a step closer to ensuring my presence in my son's life. The process was long and arduous, but giving up was never an option. I had faced enemies before, but none as challenging as this. Yet, I knew that the bond between a father and son was worth every battle scar. In the end, the struggle was not just about winning a legal case; it was about securing a foundation of love and support for my child.

The battles I fought, both on the battlefield and in the courtroom, were all for him. They were all for the moments we would share, the lessons I would teach him, and the love that would guide him through his own life. And so, with unwavering resolve, I continued to fight, knowing that my greatest victory was yet to come—the victory of being a father to my son.

Here's the biggest struggle of being a single parent. Most parents must have experienced waking up at least once in the night by their child, changing their diaper, getting them a milk bottle, or simply just waking up to them randomly crying. When Jaxon was with me, I was always so nervous as I didn't want anything bad to happen to him on my watch, and I wanted to do all I could for him, but I had no other support. In those time periods, it was just me and my son navigating our challenges together. Life as a single father with no other guidance was tough, but I somehow made it through.

I remember those nights when he kept crying because he was too young to express what he was feeling. For the first two years, Jaxon cried a lot, and I later found out that it was due to colicky, a symptom in children with autism. They don't know how to express that they are in pain or unease, so all they can do is cry. My nights became a constant of rocking him to sleep, holding him close and trying to lull him, and doing anything possible to stop him from crying. So, for the time that I had my son, I didn't sleep at all, staying awake to look after him and making sure that he wasn't in any discomfort.

The arrangement between Jaxon's mother and I continued until 2018 when I was allowed to keep my son with me for the weekends and a night each week. However, by the end of 2018, we figured out that Jaxon was a little behind on speech and social cues. He had turned two that year, but we had that sinking feeling that something was wrong with him.

Chapter 5: Second Deployment

"To be prepared for war is one of the most effective means of preserving peace."

—*George Washington*

In June 2018, I received a notification informing me that I had to leave for Afghanistan for my second deployment. Being in the Air Force, it was expected that we had signed a contract and knew we would be deployed whenever the need arose.

However, the first time I was deployed, I feared stepping into the unknown. I felt my second time wouldn't be so bad, but I was proved wrong because leaving Jaxon behind was the hardest part. I might not have been afraid of the war, but I feared leaving and never coming back to see my boy. I feared missing out on the important parts of his life, and as most of his early years had been spent with his mother and me battling for his custody, I did not want to sacrifice the hard-earned time I had received with him.

For a soldier, his duty to the country comes first and foremost. So, I knew there was nothing I could do to stop myself, and I had to respond to the call.

According to my orders, I had to be shipped out in August of 2018 to Kandahar Air Base in Afghanistan. Trump was in office by then, and I thought the war would end soon as he was slowing down bombing missions and winding things up. Thus, I had the conviction that it wouldn't be as tough as my first deployment. All I had to do was play my part and return safely to my son.

The day came for me to leave, so I packed my bags and said goodbye to Jaxon at the airport. I kissed his forehead as I knew I wouldn't be able to see him for a long time. I held back tears because all my life, I had thought I was a tough man and had to act like one. I felt I had built up enough resilience to take on anything fate threw at me. But at that moment, I realized that despite my resilience and strength, the pain of parting with loved ones is no different from a golf club aimed at your shin.

However, I got on the plane and transitioned from the father leaving his son behind to a soldier going to fight for his country. Unlike my first time, I was prepared and knew what was expected of me. I was mentally prepared to land with my gun and body armor, ready to serve in any way required of me.

I knew as soon as we landed, I would get off and be mortared or attacked. In a war situation, we seldom get to keep track of time. All we get is the soldier's minute, and it could be our last. Thus, I knew what I had to do and was resolute to give my all for the sake of my country.

We landed at a stand, and I spent three months there. My first week was similar to the first week of my previous deployment. But after those seven days, we were trained for our mission ahead. We had no days off and worked twelve-hour shifts, learning how to load our aircraft and how to complete our mission. We had to fight the Taliban and take out their resources as our primary mission. But as it was almost the end of the war, we knew we weren't going to go toe to toe with the Taliban; we were just meeting them economically.

The whole time I was there, I knew my mind was supposed to be invested in the mission, and I had to be there mentally and physically, but all I could think about was my boy. Transitioning from your personal life to the mindset of a soldier is never a complete process. Some part of you still longs for the family you left behind and the people who are waiting for you. You simply can't cut them out of your thoughts and feelings.

After seven days in the base, I was finally able to Facetime Jaxon for about twenty minutes every other day if the WiFi was working properly. He was just two and a half years old when I was deployed and hadn't learned to speak yet. So, when I called, his mother would pick up and answer. I used to schedule my calls because I felt that if I spared twenty minutes and called, what would happen if she didn't pick up? Those twenty minutes would go to waste, and I wouldn't get to see my son anytime soon.

Furthermore, it was hard with Jaxon not being vocal as each time I called, his mother would give him the phone, and even though he recognized me, he didn't say anything. The smile on his face was proof that he recognized his Dad, but other than that, I had no audible proof that he was happy to see me and wanted to talk to me. I wanted to hear him say,

"Oh, look, it's Daddy." But as he wasn't speaking, I couldn't see that wish come to fruition.

Still, that smile on his face each time I called gave me the strength to move on through those three months. Through each challenge and hardship I faced, I thought of my son and pictured that smile on his face. Thus, it motivated me to get through every passing day so that I could make it back to my family safe and sound.

Just knowing that he could see me and recognize me each time I was able to Facetime him made me feel like I hadn't left him behind. A part of him was still with me in the form of his memories.

Although the WiFi was bad and Facetiming someone in the other corner of the world had its own limitations, I still felt grateful that I had joined the military at a time when we had the technology to connect with our loved ones. If I had joined in the early 2000s or the time before that, say a hundred years ago, then I would not even have the opportunity to see my family and talk to them while I was deployed. I might have received only a letter or a care package once a month. Thus, I feel so blessed to live in a time when technology has bridged the gap between us and our loved ones despite the miles of geographical distance separating us.

Here, I want to give a shout-out to all those veterans who went to war and were disconnected completely from their families and lives back home. They never got to talk and see their kids and wives until they returned home. Thinking about it makes me salute their mental resilience and the sacrifices they made for the sake of their country.

So, I missed Jaxon, but I was able to talk to him for twenty minutes every other day. During those times, we weren't getting mortared or attacked as often as we were back in my first deployment. So once every week or so, we would face a mortar attack. The first time I had been mortared, I hit the ground at the sound of the siren, and my mind panicked, thoughts whirling in my head as if I was looking death right in the face. But until my second and third time, I was no longer panicked.

I had simply gotten accustomed to it. The sound of the siren didn't send us into a frenzy, and instead of getting down quickly, we felt it was just another day, which was our kind of normal. We knew by then how inaccurate the aim was when we were being mortared, so we would slowly get down, wait for a few minutes, and then walk back to our shelters and wait there until the attacks stopped.

It is crazy when you think about how you can form mental resilience against the most extreme of experiences if you have been through them more often. And if you talk to the veterans, they will tell you the same thing that the more you experience it, you get kind of numb to everything happening around you. It no longer scares you or sends you into a panic because you have made it through it multiple times before.

It's like going to work and experiencing what you expect to happen at your job. For instance, if you are a mechanic, you get used to fixing cars such that a smoke-erupting engine no longer bothers you. Similarly, if you are a soldier or in a constant situation of war, you get accustomed to mortars flying over your head and staying away from your family for long periods of time. You almost get numb to it.

It was three weeks into my deployment when we got attacked. At that time, my friend and I were loading an aircraft and getting it ready for its next mission. The sirens went off, and we saw an explosion in the distance. I remember looking at the explosion and then at my friend as we were casually walking away to the shelter.

Despite the smoke and the explosion, we looked at each other and smiled. It was kind of crazy that we were men at war and anything could happen to us at any given moment, but we were so desensitized to it that it felt almost a normal occurrence. Any other person would have panicked in that situation, but we had gotten accustomed to it, so it didn't faze us anymore.

The shelters where we were supposed to wait until the attack ended were made out of concrete and about fifty feet long to cram as many soldiers inside as possible. These shelters were essentially three slabs of concrete with two standing vertically as pillars and one slab balanced on them horizontally. We were all crammed inside and had to wait for hours until the attacks ended, and it was safe to come out again.

Being crammed with about fifty people, it was difficult to even breathe, but the worst part was when I would feel something crawling on my leg. I had a fear of bugs, and during my first deployment, I brought a bug net with me. But in the second deployment, I didn't bring it because I thought I could face that fear. However, while we were in the shelter, I felt something crawling up my leg. My first thought was that it had to be some bug. I wanted to scream and jump, but I knew I couldn't do so in front of all those soldiers crammed in with me.

So, I looked at my leg and saw a big spider. I remember my heart racing as I kind of brushed it to the ground. But all the while, I was thinking, "Oh God, I am not going to die from a mortar attack but from a bloody spider bite." Fear affects us in multiple ways, and I remember thinking that if the spider bit me, my leg might fall off. But I had to put up with it because once a week, we got mortared, and then we had to stay in the shelter until the attack subsided. Of course, it had spiders, some of which could be as big as your hand.

In Afghanistan and the Middle East, we also get to encounter camel spiders. These spiders are large and hairy and almost look like crabs. I had an encounter with one of these spiders, which scared the crap out of me.

It was about 11 pm, and our jets had just landed and came back with no ammunition on them. So, we had four hours to get those jets reloaded and refueled. A team of three, including me, went out to reload the jet. I got the ammo out there; I had my team and my toolbox, and everything was good to go.

We had a little bit of light there and came out fifteen minutes prior to ammo. So, we were sitting there and talking to each other casually about the gym and whatnot when I suddenly heard a pounding sound. It was like you took your fingers and drummed them at the desk; it was so distinct.

I asked my companions if they could hear that sound, too, but they didn't. I could have passed it off as a superstition, but I heard the sound again, and it was louder than it had been earlier. A camel spider the size of my hand ran full speed at me and collided with my boot. As I looked down at it, it seemed as if the spider had made eye contact with me. I was startled, so I jumped, and the people around me started laughing. When I looked down again, the spider had taken off, vanishing into the night.

To this day, I wonder why that spider chose to run at me only, even though there were about seven people around me. It was almost as if the spider knew I would be afraid of it and chose to launch itself at me.

While we were at the Kandahar Air Base, the Taliban and the local Afghan government settled on a ceasefire that lasted about four weeks. During that ceasefire, we were also not going to blow anything up or affect the local government and their agreement with the Taliban. So, for the time being, it felt as if the war was already over. During those four weeks of the ceasefire, we frequented the Morale Welfare and Recreation Place that we called MWR. For six hours a day, we would go there and play ping pong and darts. I even bought an eighty-dollar paddle for ping pong and had it shaped all the way over to Afghanistan by Amazon. It was bizarre as we were in the ceasefire, knowing we had to be ready to go to war once it ended, yet we were playing ping pong and darts.

I got really good at both the games, like how Forrest Gump mastered ping pong in his time in the military. But in hindsight, I still missed my son and wanted to go back home soon. The only thing that kept me going was hope for a better future and an assurance that I would get to see my son again once I completed my second deployment and returned to my country successfully.

In this deployment, I was given a leadership position, so I gave all my fellows twenty minutes a day to contact their families because I knew how hard it was to do our duty at the border miles away from home. We couldn't let our feelings and emotions deter our performance in the military, so it was better to have a fixed time to talk with the family and tell them that we were doing alright.

I feel that none of us really talk about our problems with each other, and that stigma needs to change. Talking about our problems and challenges makes them real, but it also gives us the strength to face them and move ahead. You must have heard the saying that when a buffalo sees a storm, it charges at the storm and walks through it, while most herd animals tend to run away from it. If you walk through the storm, you are in it for only a few minutes. But if you run away from the storm, it lingers over you like an impending doom for quite a long time.

I wanted to be like the bull that charges at the storm and makes it through. Why can't we, as a society, be taught that we have to face our problems instead of running away from them? Why can't we all be like the bulls charging at the storm and emerging triumphant on the other side?

I knew I was in Afghanistan so far away from my son, and I couldn't get to see him daily; that was my biggest problem. But instead of running away, I braced myself to make the best out of my situation so that, in the end, I could return to my son with my head held high. So, I wanted to spread the message that let's talk about all our problems, make them real, and get past them.

My second war deployment was a bit easier in that aspect. I had built up my mental resilience, and like the bull, I knew I could charge at the storm. The short disconnect we felt was during the four weeks of ceasefire when we were not in action. In those days, I hit the gym a lot to regulate my mood and keep myself grounded. You know how they say that if you need to take out your frustration and elevate your mood, go to the gym. Similarly, I spent hours at the gym to keep myself sane and functional.

Going to the gym regularly, I made it my mission to get into the thousand-pound club. For that, we had to flat bench, do squats, and do deadlifts, and if the sum of these three lifts was over a thousand pounds, then we got a thousand-pound lift. If we did the lifts in front of the person who operated the MWR, he would give us a shirt and write our names on the leaderboard. So, I made that my target and had to practice it for four weeks.

I worked hard and lifted over a thousand and five pounds. The man at the MWR shook my hand and put my name on the leaderboard along with ten other guys who had made it to the thousand-pound club. But I didn't get to have the shirt because the last of them was given to a guy who went before me. He was one of the weapon guys and worked alongside me. However, his three lifts combined only made about 960 pounds, while I had lifted over a thousand. So, I resented that he got the last shirt due to a mathematical error, but I didn't get it despite all my hard work. To this day, I serve that guy, and I remind him of that incident by calling him Mister 1000.

Two weeks before we were supposed to go home, the mortar attacks started again. The ceasefire had ended, and we got attacked. But by then, we knew we had made it that far, so we simply had to persevere and make it through those attacks as well. We felt a lot of pressure, but the relief of going home soon motivated us to move on and spend the remaining two weeks at the base doing our tasks and facing those attacks.

We all did it, and it felt amazing to leave the base and head home to our country. As the plane took off, I had only one thought in my head that I did it and made it through my second deployment. The storm was finally over, and I would get to see Jaxon again.

On the way home, we had to do a stopover in Germany. We were three hundred military guys, and we literally drank the airport out of liquor and beer. We stayed there for only three hours, but in our ecstasy of returning from the war, we drank heavily until there was no liquor left at the airport. If you ever go drinking with a military guy, you should know that they can handle their liquor very well and know how to drink heavily.

Finally, we got home, and the first thing I did was drive all the way to Indiana to pick up my boy from his mother's place. That feeling was overwhelming as I couldn't wait to lay eyes on him and hug him tightly. I had missed him a lot, and every second felt like a stretch of time apart from him that I couldn't wait to get rid of. When I got to him, it was like a scene straight out of a movie. I ran to him, and he was so delighted to see me that he ran toward me as well. I lifted him up in my arms, and I don't think I let go of hugging him for about an hour or so.

Holding him in my arms was the feeling that confirmed for me that I was at home and back with my boy. He was so excited that he cried and held onto me tightly. I wouldn't give up that memory for anything, and it is still fresh in my mind—the utter joy and relief I felt from being able to see him and hug him again.

Chapter 6: The Puzzle Piece

"Autism is not a processing error. It's a different operating system."

—Sarah Hendrickx

Autism Spectrum Disorder (ASD) is a complicated condition that impacts brain development and changes an individual's perception and interaction with their surrounding environment. This developmental disorder typically manifests in childhood, though the timing and nature of its symptoms can vary widely.

No two individuals with autism are exactly alike, but they often share challenges in social communication, exhibit repetitive behaviors, and have intense, focused interests. ASD affects social interaction, communication, and behavior, leading to notable difficulties in daily life. Sometimes, symptoms of autism can be observed in babies. A baby may fail to establish eye contact, acknowledge their name, or exhibit curiosity towards their caretakers.

As the child grows, these signs may become more pronounced. They may exhibit repetitive behaviors, possess a narrow scope of interests, or respond strangely to sensory stimuli such as light, sound, or texture. Other children with autism might develop typically at first, meeting milestones like speaking their first words or engaging in play with others. Suddenly, without warning, they might start to decline, forgetting abilities they had previously mastered.

This decline can be upsetting for both the child and those who take care of them, as the previously lively and talkative child becomes isolated, uncommunicative, or even hostile.

Around the age of two, most signs of autism become more noticeable. Some autistic children might have difficulties engaging in social communication, especially when it comes to interpreting nonverbal cues like tone of voice, facial gestures, and body language. They might have difficulty forming friendships or engaging in imaginative play, preferring instead to stick to rigid routines or focus intently on specific interests.

The degree of autism can differ widely from person to person, with some being nonverbal or needing substantial help in daily tasks and others being highly functional, living on their own, and having exceptional abilities in certain areas. Some children with autism may have intellectual disabilities, making learning difficult and impacting their ability to communicate effectively.

However, some individuals exhibit typical or higher intelligence levels despite facing obstacles. These kids frequently shine in academic environments, learning subjects rapidly, but may find it challenging to use their knowledge in social situations or adjust to new surroundings. Each child who has autism is special, showing a unique mix of abilities and difficulties. For some, the journey includes learning to communicate in ways that may not come naturally, while for others, it involves navigating the complexities of social relationships or finding ways to manage sensory sensitivities.

Some autistic people need to work on their communication skills, while others struggle with social relationships or sensory sensitivities. Despite the difficulties that may arise, many individuals with autism lead fulfilling lives, especially when given the appropriate support and opportunities to thrive. Understanding the spectrum of autism is crucial in providing the right care and fostering an environment where every child can reach their full potential.

Through my personal experience of raising an autistic child, I can say for certain that it is not a disorder. I prefer thinking of it as a lens that enables the people affected by it to view the world differently from others. Some autistic individuals are nonverbal, while others are highly articulate. Some struggle with sensory overload, finding everyday sounds and textures overwhelming, while others might seek out intense sensory experiences.

My journey with accepting autism started when I returned from my second deployment. Compared to my first deployment, I was better prepared for the readjustment period and knew how to fit back into the normal life that I had left behind. Thus, I knew it would take time to get back into the swing of things and to bridge the communication gap with my family. However, I wasn't prepared for the nagging feeling that something wasn't quite right with my son, Jaxon.

Jaxon turned three in 2019, and it was around that time we began to notice something unsettling. He was lagging behind on social skills, not engaging with other children, and still behaving as if he were much younger than his actual age. He wasn't interested in the same toys or activities that captivated other kids. While his peers were beginning to communicate, form friendships, and explore the world with a growing sense of independence, Jaxon remained in his own bubble, content yet distant.

Once a month, we would visit my dad at his place, which had a little farm, a barn, a pool, and some four-wheelers. Back then, I took Jaxon with me so that he could enjoy playing with his cousins, but I noticed that his behavior was much different compared to other children. It seemed Jaxon was there physically, but he wasn't quite there mentally, as he was rather unresponsive. His cousins are around his age, as one of them is six years younger than him, and the other is a year younger than Jaxon. But his behavior was strikingly different from them. I also tried calling his name at times, but he didn't answer, as though he either didn't recognize his name or couldn't hear me.

Concerned for my son, I discussed it with his mother, and at first, we thought it might be a hearing issue. Maybe he just couldn't hear us calling his name, which would explain why he often seemed disconnected or unresponsive. Perhaps he could not hear us over the noise, or something was wrong with his auditory senses. I remember the day we took him to get his hearing checked, hoping for a fixable solution. But when the results showed his hearing was perfectly normal, we were left with more questions than ever. The problem lay elsewhere, and that realization set us on a path we hadn't anticipated.

We didn't know what was wrong with our son, which worried us equally. His hearing was perfect, but his responses were somewhat off. We spoke to Jaxon's primary care doctor a couple of months later about the situation. She suggested we have him checked out by a specialist at Peyton Manning Children's Hospital in Indianapolis, mentioning that it could be possible that Jaxon was autistic.

Hearing the specialist's advice, I felt like my world had come to a stop. Not my son, the words echoed in my head. I felt there had been some mistake because how could Jaxon, with my genetics, be on the spectrum? I had always excelled at sports and prided myself on my intelligence, knowing my son would be just like me. In fact, I had it in mind that he would grow up to be an all-star linebacker. There couldn't be anything wrong with my kid.

However, I began to immerse myself in research about autism, especially in young children. I poured over articles, books, and online forums, desperately trying to understand what might be going on with Jaxon. I soon discovered that autism is not a one-size-fits-all condition—it manifests differently in every child. The more I learned, the more I began to see the signs in Jaxon—his difficulty with eye contact, his fascination with certain objects, and his need for routine. It became evident that Jaxon wasn't ignoring us—he simply processed the world in his own unique way.

So, Jaxon's mother and I took him to Peyton Manning Hospital and met with a specialist, a woman whose gentle demeanor put me at ease even as I braced myself for what was to come. After a thorough evaluation—one that included observations, questions about Jaxon's behavior, and a series of tests—the diagnosis was made: Jaxon had autism.

I'll never forget the moment those words were spoken—it felt like the ground had been pulled out from beneath me. My heart sank, and a wave of emotions hit me like a tidal wave. I remember holding Jaxon as the doctor explained his condition to us. She told us that four things made Jaxon autistic. His sensory abilities were a little off; he got bothered by too much light and a lot of noise, and he didn't understand any social cues.

For the next week, I cried more than I had in years. My mind raced with fears and questions: *What if he is never a successful adult? What if he never grows out of this? What if kids pick on him when I'm not there? What if he needs to be in a special needs class?*

On the other hand, Jaxon was as happy as ever, blissfully unaware that anything had changed. But for me, everything had changed. My world was flipped upside down.

As a single father, I felt so alone. Who could I call for help? What was I supposed to do? I was trying to raise Jaxon to the best of my ability, but with his diagnosis, I felt as if I was standing alone in the face of adversity. Despite being deployed two times and facing the war head-on, I knew this was nothing like my past experiences. It required a different kind of emotional strength and endurance so that I could work with my son and help him adjust to the world.

But here's what I want other parents to know: if your child is diagnosed with autism, it's not the end of the world. You have plenty of options that you can explore, but the first thing you have to do is gain understanding and awareness. So, we had an hour-and-a-half-long debriefing session with the specialist at Peyton Manning Hospital about what we needed to do next.

She gave us a six-page checklist of the next steps: file for Medicaid, get him into occupational and speech therapy, and so much more. It was overwhelming, but I knuckled down and started working through that list. The first step is acceptance because when you accept the problem, you start thinking about how you should tackle it. So, acceptance was key for me, and when I came to terms with my own fears regarding my son, I realized that I had a lot to do for him and that I should get started as soon as possible.

Just like the bull that heads toward the storm, I accepted my son as he was and started working on giving him everything he deserved, including an opportunity to be understood. We immediately sought out an occupational therapist and a speech therapist to start working with Jaxon, hoping to help him catch up to other kids his age. As time passed, we accepted that it was not a sudden fix and that it would require time and effort on our part as well for Jaxon to show signs of improvement.

For the first six months of therapy, we didn't see much progress. There were days when it felt like we were fighting an uphill battle with no end in sight. But the specialists kept reminding us to believe in the milestones and understand that every little step was a conquest, and it would all happen in Jaxon's timeframe. Instead of forcing Jaxon to be a fully functioning normal kid, we were advised to look at the situation from a different perspective and modify our expectations accordingly. Not all children are alike, so comparing my son to others was futile. Instead, I had to understand things from his perspective and continue supporting him.

We set up a strict routine that included daily therapy sessions, exercises at home, and constant encouragement. I remember the first time Jaxon said a full sentence—it was a simple request for a snack, but to me, it felt like he had moved a mountain. We celebrated that moment as if he had just won an Olympic gold medal, as it was a definite step in the right direction and proved that all our hard work hadn't gone in vain.

Still, public outings were the hardest for Jaxon. The anxiety I felt every time we went out was overwhelming. It seemed like all eyes were on us, judging us, and it was painfully clear that our family didn't fit into the normal mold. Jaxon's struggles with sensory overload, his meltdowns, and his inability to engage with others in a typical way drew stares, and I felt the weight of those inquisitive eyes with every step we took. Often, I questioned everything: *Why was this happening to us? Would things ever get better? Would Jaxon ever have a chance at a normal life?*

I vividly recall one particular outing to a grocery store. Jaxon had a meltdown in the middle of the aisle, overwhelmed by the bright lights and the noise. People stared, some with pity, others with annoyance. My heart raced, my palms sweated, and I fought back tears as I tried to soothe him, feeling helpless and exposed. In those moments, I realized how isolating this journey could be— how easy it was for others to judge when they didn't understand what we were going through. But looking back now, those two to three years when he really started to make progress were some of the most transformative of my life. Slowly but surely, Jaxon began to emerge from his shell.

Watching Jaxon grow into the talented eight-year-old he is today has been incredible, but it hasn't always been easy. Taking him to the grocery store or the playground was a challenge because they thought he was weird when he interacted with other children. It was heart-wrenching for me to see him avoid making eye contact and be silent in the company of other kids his age. Making friends was also hard for him until the age of seven because he couldn't pick up on social cues and behaved differently. I knew I had to do something about it because a life without friends or peers who you can rely on is rather difficult. I didn't want my boy to miss out on the benefits offered by friendship.

I made it my mission to teach him social skills. I told him I understood it was weird and awkward for him to get to know kids, promising him I would help him. When he was six and in kindergarten, he came to me saying none of the kids would play with him. So, I taught him that the first step was to introduce himself, shake hands, and ask simple questions like "What's your favorite color?"

Jaxon tried doing that, but he would mess it up for a year straight. Sometimes, he would shake his left hand instead of his right; other times, he would forget names and not reply immediately. But now, after all the practice, he has finally gotten the hang of it. Now, he can walk up to anyone and strike up a conversation with him. He introduces himself and asks for their name, and often, the conversation diverts to Mario or Sonic. But he has overcome the disconnect he felt earlier with other children of his age.

After two years of therapy—and Jaxon's still in therapy today for behavior and social cues—I have come to realize something profound: I don't even know what normal is anymore. Growing up, I thought I was a normal kid, but now I have realized that normal is subjective and different from every other person. We all perceive this world differently, right? Raising my son Jaxon, I feel like I've done so much growing myself as a parent and a person. I have realized that he experiences the world in a unique way—it's not abnormal, just different.

I feel like Jaxon collects more data than a neurotypical person. He sees more, hears more, and understands more—it just takes him longer to process it all before making a decision. Getting to know my son and understanding how he perceives the world has made a lot of difference for me, too. When you are raising someone with autism, it is very important to accept that you can't expect them to conform to your idea of normal. You have to step into their shoes and see the world through their eyes. Once you can do that, they truly start making progress.

Thus, I accepted with my full heart that my son would grow up and be Jaxon Glad, the man he wanted to be, and all I could do was help guide him. I've tried to put a set standard on what he should be, but now that he has autism, he's into video games, he loves swimming, and he's growing up to be his own person, so I should accept him for his most authentic self rather than implement a version of normal over him.

I believe that I got lucky with Jaxon. He's been re-diagnosed on the mild spectrum now because he has gained so many skills that he was lacking between ages three and five. I know there are more severe cases out there, and every person with autism is different. You must understand and embrace their uniqueness instead of labeling autism as a disorder. Through Jaxon, I realized that to overcome the stigma of autism, we all have to work as a supportive community and provide autistic individuals with the best assistance and understanding. As parents, caregivers, friends, and family members, we play a crucial role in the lives of people on the spectrum. Instead of disregarding them, we should accept their differences and integrate them as well as we possibly can.

It wasn't an easy journey as we understood Jaxon's autism and supported him. We faced many setbacks along the way, but the progress over time was undeniable. And with that progress, something incredible happened: I began to see the world through Jaxon's eyes. We started to build memories during that time—memories that no other parent has. Every small victory, every moment of connection, felt like a shared triumph. We experienced life differently from other parents and normal kids, and while that difference once felt like a burden, it eventually became something I cherished. Jaxon taught me to see the world in a new light, appreciate the little things, and find joy in moments others might overlook.

The key for any parent with a child with autism is finding their wheelhouse—what they're interested in. It can be dinosaurs, trains, or video games. It can simply be a passion that intrigues your child and keeps him invested. Let them sink into it fully. For Jaxon, this passion is Sonic and Mario. Our whole house is covered in Sonic and Mario merchandise. This summer, we went to Universal Studios, spending ten hours in the Super Nintendo World dedicated to Mario, Jaxon's favorite video game character. He loved every second of it and still talks about it.

So, to other single parents out there, to parents who have autistic children: dive into what your kids love. Pour your heart and soul into it with them. Embrace the small victories, build on them, and witness your child blossom into their distinct and amazing self. The journey may not be what you anticipated, but I assure you, it's one hell of a ride.

The journey from that initial diagnosis to today has been filled with challenges, tears, and moments of doubt. But it's also been a journey of love, growth, and unexpected joys.

Autism isn't an obstacle; it's a different path. It's taught me patience I never knew I had and opened my eyes to a world of details I had never noticed before. Connecting with Jaxon and understanding him has given me a deeper appreciation for the small victories in life.

My boy may not be the all-star linebacker I once imagined, but he is something far more precious. He's uniquely and wonderfully himself, and I love him for who he is, not for who he should be.

Chapter 7: Life Goes On

"I am prepared for the worst but hope for the best."

—Benjamin Disraeli

In the silent hours of the night, after the world has settled and my son has fallen asleep, I often sit alone and reflect on the life I have built. When I look at Jaxon peacefully asleep, I know that every struggle I went through has been worth it. I faced wars, stayed away from my family, struggled with my relationships, and spent a long time of my life battling for my son's custody, but in the end, everything fell into place just like it was supposed to.

Now, I am with my son and leading my life as a single father, constantly walking the tightrope between being a protector, provider, and nurturer all at once. Each day brought new challenges that I turned into opportunities to show my son what love, strength, and true resilience really look like. None of this could have been possible without mental resilience and the determination to face my challenges head-on.

Looking back at these past few years, I realize this wasn't the life I had planned for, but it has become the life I would never give up for anything. As I look back, I think that when we are 18 to 21 years old, we spread our wings and learn to fly in the vast skies of our practical life. At that time, becoming a father had not been on my list, but once I accepted it, I decided to be the best father I could be for my son.

Even on the hardest days, when exhaustion weighs me down and doubts creep in, I remind myself that while I may be doing this alone, my child would never have to feel the same way as I would always be there for him. My deepest wish for him is to be able to stand with him when things are hard and to provide him with unconditional love and support.

Fatherhood is tough; there's no denying it. But I know that the love I am giving him is pure, and he appreciates everything I do for him. My past has definitely shaped me just like it does with everyone else, but I have refused to let it define me anymore.

The journey of healing has been the hardest I have ever embarked on, but it is the most powerful thing I have ever done for myself. I faced the darkness of my past, and now, I stand in the light of my future, being stronger and more resilient than ever.

In other words, what once broke me down has now become the foundation of my strength. The scars of my past are no longer etched upon my soul, and I do not recall them as painful memories. Instead, they have become the symbols of my resilience. All our scars never really go away, but they come to mean something much more than just signifying the perils we experienced. I see my scars as proof of my mental resilience. These scars depict that I survived everything through my mental resilience.

As a veteran, I know full well how war can change a person. True, I have left parts of myself on the battlefield, but I've returned with a deeper appreciation for life. Each deployment had taken a piece of me, but it also taught me the true meaning of sacrifice.

First, I fought for my country, but after returning from my second deployment, my battle was to find peace within myself. I was trained to be a warrior—doing God's work for my country. However, I realized the battle still existed after my return, but now it was just within me.

I had seen the worst of humanity had to offer, but I also witnessed the best in my brothers and sisters in arms. Thus, deployment definitely tested my limits, but it showed me a strength I never knew I had.

After returning home from my deployment, I immediately had to step into another battle, which I recall as the battle for justice. I fought not just for my rights but for my son's right to know his father. Justice was elusive, and the system seemed to be against me, but my love for my son was unwavering and enabled me to stand tough in front of all the storms in my way.

They tried to silence me—the system, the court, the lawyers—but I believe a father's voice cannot be ignored. The battle for custody was long and unjust, yet my commitment to my son has never wavered and never will. Being up against a system that sought to break me, my resolve only grew stronger. In the face of corruption, I chose to stand firm because my son deserved to know his father as a person and a strong support for him. He deserved to spend time with the man who was equally responsible for bringing him into the world and wanted to contribute as much as possible to his life. I believe every single father should have that right.

Raising my son, who is on the autism spectrum, has been a journey of its own. It is strikingly different from the battle of custody, so I would never weigh the two on the same scale. But every challenge was an opportunity to show my son that he was perfect, being his true self.

My son's autism doesn't define him, and I don't want to change him. I feel like a lot of people think there is something wrong with their children when they are diagnosed with autism. Initially, when I had no experience and awareness, I thought the same way—as if it was something I had to fix. But now that I have seen him grow and accept himself, I don't want to change anything about him. Instead, I want to understand him better with every passing day. In short, raising a child with autism has taught me more about love, patience, and resilience than all my other battles ever could.

My son sees the world differently, and that's what makes him extraordinary in my eyes. I wasn't just teaching Jaxon how to navigate the world. In fact, he was teaching me to see the world in a new light. In short, for everything that I have taught him so far, he has taught me tenfold. Through him, I learned the true meaning of resilience.

In a world that tried to break me, I have discovered that my mind is the greatest weapon. I used to think that physical fitness was the key to staying strong—my military training also emphasized that. But now I have realized that being strong means having resilience in four aspects: physical, mental, emotional, and spiritual. Thus, I have built my resilience on these four pillars.

The way I see it, resilience isn't about never falling. It is about rising stronger each time you fall. I used to chase perfection, and I feared failure. But now, I've realized it's not how you fall or when you fall because everyone's going to fall sooner or later. What matters is whether you get stronger every time you fall. Strength isn't just physical power—it is the ability to keep going when everything inside you wants to stop.

I faced all my storms, and just like a bull runs headfirst through the storm, I faced the storms within my mind as well. Facing these challenges, I feel like I've emerged with a deeper understanding of my own power.

My resilience was never about being invincible because no one can achieve that. Instead, it was focused on being unbreakable. The simplest way to understand it is to be like water. Bruce Lee also mentions, *"Be like water making its way through cracks. Do not be assertive, but adjust to the object, and you shall find a way around or through it. You put water into a bottle; it becomes the bottle. You put it in a teapot; it becomes the teapot. Water can flow, or it can crash. Be water, my friend."*

One of the most important lessons I have learned in life that I wish to share with you is that strength isn't in facing everything alone. In fact, it is knowing when to reach out. This book is strictly written to give other people the ability to reach out and seek help. That was my primary purpose in writing this book and sharing my story with the world. If I can help one person get the mental resilience and the strength they need to reach out for help, then it is all worth it.

I want you to know and accept that asking for help doesn't make you weak. It certainly didn't weaken me. I had to learn that true courage lies in admitting when you need a hand. I think we all feel that we can carry the weight on our shoulders, but we never know when too much weight is too much for us until we collapse. I used to think asking for help was a sign of weakness, but now I know it's a sign of growth.

Amid our strengths and vulnerability, asking for help is the most powerful act of self-care that anyone can give themselves. I feel like there is a stigma that men can't reach out. They can't show themselves as weak. But asking for help is not a sign of weakness, and it definitely doesn't mean that you are giving up. Instead, it is a sign that you are stepping up to take control of your life. You are actually doing something and taking the right step by acknowledging that you can be stronger with the people close to you supporting you.

I have broken this stigma by reaching out for help, and through this acceptance, I have realized that seeking help was a path to healing, not a sign of defeat. My journey has been filled with battles, both external and internal. But through it all, I have emerged stronger, wiser, and more grateful. I have fought for my country, I have fought for my son, and I finally have fought for my own peace of mind.

Sitting here beside my son and knowing that he is sleeping peacefully every night and wakes up each morning ready to have an adventurous day assures me that every struggle I have been through was worth it. I might be a single father, but together, my son and I are a team—one that nothing and no one can break.

As I close this chapter of my life and this book, I realize that the term *"Millennial Warrior"* has taken on a whole new meaning for me. Once, it meant being a soldier, fighting battles in far-off lands for my country. Now, it means being a warrior every day—for my son, for myself, and for others who face similar challenges.

In my life, and especially as a single father raising a boy with autism, being a warrior isn't about victory in combat anymore. It's about the daily victories—helping Jaxon tie his shoelaces, watching him make a friend at the park, or seeing him master a new skill we've been working on for months. It is about fighting against a system that doesn't always understand and accommodate neurodiversity. It is about battling my own demons from the past while striving to be the best father I can be.

So, to my fellow Millennial Warriors—whether you are veterans, parents, or both—I want you to know that our battles may be different now, but they are no less important.

We have the power to shape the future for our children, to break cycles of trauma, to accept our children as their authentic selves, and to redefine what strength really means.

As for Jaxon and me, our journey is far from over. We have a lot to see and experience in life together, and a million adventures and new battles await us. But we would never back down from the challenges in store as we are each other's strength. In this journey of love, growth, and understanding, we march forward as two warriors, hand in hand, ready to face whatever life brings our way.

MILLENNIAL WARRIOR

Jack Randall Glad

Chapter 1: Mental Resilience

"Resilience embodies the personal qualities that enable one to thrive in the face of adversity."

—Kathryn Connor

They say millennials were the generation that was promised the world; they opened their eyes at a time when technology was advancing, and the future held great hope. But then, as they lived on, they fell prey to some of the worst calamities, watching their promised world of dreams and ambitions crumble.

Being a millennial and witnessing these calamities firsthand, I agree with this claim and speak on behalf of my generation.

We were digital pioneers raised on optimism and the promise of a bright future—a transitional generation hoping to enter a different reality with the dawn of the 21st Century.

But the world had other plans that did not align with our soaring ambitions.

Most of us were still young enough to process the changing dynamics of the world when we were hit by the tragedy of 9/11. We also lived through the recession of 2001, followed shortly by the 2008 Great Recession. By the time we stepped into our practical lives, our shoulders were weighed down by college debt, and jobs were scarce. Thus, we were all competing in the gritting race to secure the rare white-collar jobs.

Milton Keynes UK
Ingram Content Group UK Ltd.
UKHW020725121124
451038UK00018B/325